SHERE CHUR

A HISTORY

By Eric Thornton

*Dear Nellie
with best wishes
Eric Thornton*

TWIGA BOOKS
GOMSHALL

First Published in 2008

Twiga Books
Twiga Lodge
Wonham Way
Gomshall
Guildford   GU5 9NZ

Printed by Intypelibra Ltd

ISBN 978 0 9528625 4 3

ACKNOWLEDGEMENTS

For such a little book it is surprising from how many people I have needed help. My very grateful thanks are due to the following:
To Elizabeth Rich for scouring the Shere Museum's extensive archives and bringing to my attention every mention of the bells she found. Elizabeth also raised the 'I' for 'J' problem and read the first draft, making apt comments. This on top of serving numerous cups of tea with biscuits and much encouragement. After reading the draft Ann Noyes pointed out, amongst much else, that four marks is exactly half of £5.6.8d and reminded me of the story of Reginald Bray and Richard III's crown. Ann also provided her 'Twiga Books' as publisher. Sally Reay, one of my friends in the tower and a gifted artist, did most of the line drawings and David Hicks researched the story of John Aubrey. I had seen the reverse 'N' on the inscription on the fourth bell many times but without noticing the anomaly until Jonathan Cross, the present steeple keeper, pointed it out and I then found the rest. Tim Austin kindly handed over all his paperwork relating to the preparation of the latest edition of 'History of St James' Church Shere' and John Parker, another bell ringing friend, provided the photographs of the present ringers (taken by his wife Gill) and in his capacity as churchwarden, gave me permission to use the 19th century photograph of the church interior. The Winchester and Guildford Guilds of Church Bellringers each kindly provided lists of all recorded Shere peals. The Whitechapel Bell Foundry Ltd answered all my questions promptly and gave me the story of the keynote of the Shere ring, while John E Camp gave permission for me to reproduce the cover picture from an unattributed illustration (slightly amended) from his late father's (John Camp) book 'Discovering Bells and Bellringing'. My friend Susan Pears proof read the final draft and made all sorts of sensible comments and corrections. Alan, my son, put me right about the mechanics of how a bell rings and converted my draft into book form and my wife, Norma, spent a lot of time correcting my punctuation and grammar.

St. James' Church spire and tower.

The bell chamber is immediately below the spire. The bells are housed behind the louvres. The ringers operate in the room immediately below the bell chamber; the lower window is on the north wall of the ringing chamber.

CONTENTS

Page

ILLUSTRATIONS

INTRODUCTION

It is over 20 years since I first climbed the spiral staircase to the ringing chamber to take my first lesson in bell ringing. That was the start of a fascinating and very rewarding hobby. I can't remember exactly when but after some five or six years I was talked into taking on the exalted sounding, position of 'Steeple Keeper'. The steeple keeper is responsible for ensuring the bells and associated equipment are fully functional. I was presented with a folder containing all sorts of information about bell weights, stay lengths and rope suppliers. Amongst this assortment of paperwork I came across a single sheet of foolscap paper headed 'A Short History of Shere Bells'. It was no more than a single paragraph of about 100 words followed by the weights of, and inscriptions on, the bells and had apparently been produced in the 1970s as a handout at a tower open day. The second sentence proclaimed that there were three bells in 1500. I was intrigued and wondered, why start in 1500 and when was the first bell cast? I made a mental note to investigate further. This little book is the result of that investigation, off and on, over several years.

There is a lot of literature about church bells in general but it is mostly written for, and read by, bell ringers and their ilk. Likewise, much has been written about St James' Church and Shere village but you will find precious little information about the Shere bells.

Bells have played an important part in English church history so it seems appropriate that there should be a record, however incomplete, of the history of the bells at Shere. I have included some history of the ringers as well as details of how bells ring and why English church bell ringing is so unique. I have found historical information hard to come by so in some cases it has been necessary to make assumptions. I have made plain, in the text, where such assumptions have been made and the information on which they have been based.

As the story builds over the centuries I have made an attempt to put all in perspective by referring to major national events that coincided with the story of the bells.

The parish church of St James at Shere has eight bells; that is one octave and they are in a key somewhere between E and E flat. This needs some explanation. The strike note of the tenor (the heaviest bell) vibrates at 325½ cycles per second. E International Pitch vibrates at 329½ cycles per second and E flat at 311⅛ cycles per second. Our treble was cast in the 19th century when the pitch standard was known as Old Concert Pitch. In Old Concert Pitch E vibrates at 340¼ cycles per second and E flat at 321 cycles per second. Therefore, when our last bell was cast the pitch was between E and E flat but closer to E flat but, using modern International Pitch, is between E and E flat but closer to E. Have you got that? The tenor weighs just over 15½ cwts. and the treble, the smallest bell, just over 5¼ cwts.

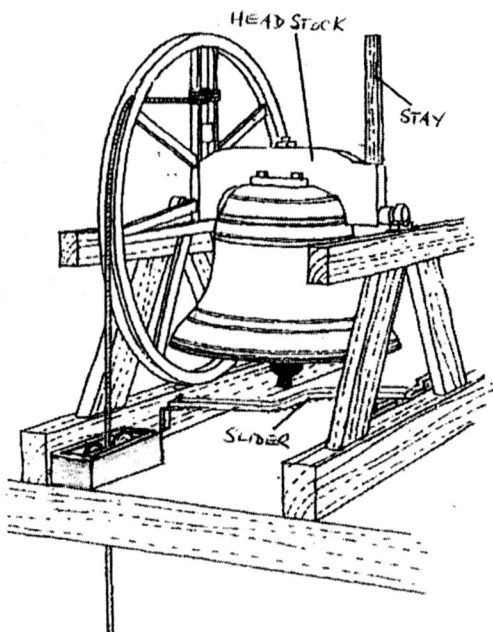

You will see from the illustration that the bell is attached to the headstock which is itself attached at one side to a large rimmed wheel. The headstock, and therefore the bell, pivots on bearings which are attached to a substantial frame. The illustration shows an iron headstock and solid oak frame, which is the configuration we have at Shere.

We will talk about the stay and slider later.

The story of our Shere bells starts some time in the 13th Century when the people of Shere added a bell chamber and a spire to their church.

13th TO 16th CENTURY

The spire can be dated to the 13th Century thanks to an inspection in 1976 by C A Hewett, an expert on timber buildings and their construction techniques. Following his inspection he wrote to the then rector, "As a result of my examination of the spire of Shere Church I am able to tell you that it must date after AD 1213 because secret notched lapjoints were used and these were incepted at Wells during the interdict. It must therefore date between 1213 and c.1300." (Presumably these secret notched lapjoints went out of use at the turn of the century.)

The spire can be dated a little more accurately as it is believed the tower was heightened to incorporate a bell chamber in c.1275. The spire sits on top of the bell chamber so the spire must also date between 1275 and 1300.

Out of interest, Hewett goes on to say, "It is the finest spire-frame I have yet seen in England." So Shere can claim the finest spire frame in England. If anyone is qualified to make such a judgement it is probably our friend C A Hewett. If you get the chance to go up to the bell loft and look up at our magnificent frame you will notice that there are dowel holes drilled which seem to have no purpose and joints cut with nothing adjoining. This probably indicates that the timbers had previously been used for something else and were second hand when the spire was built. It makes you wonder just how old the timber is – certainly more than 700 years!

You will be agog to know what a secret notched lapjoint looks like so, if you are ever in the tower, this is what you are looking for.

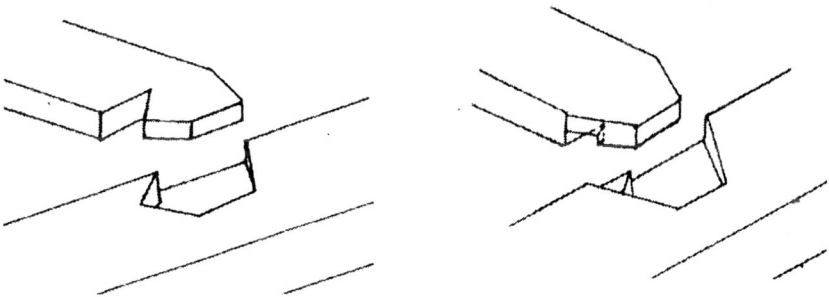

The illustration on the left shows a notched lapjoint, the one on the right shows a secret notched lapjoint. The notch is now secret because it is below the surface and you can see how it will be hidden from view.

So the spire was built in the 13th Century and it sits on top of the bell tower and ringing chamber but I can find no record of what bell or bells might have been housed in the bell tower at that time. The first record I can find for the casting of a bell is in 1513 and this appears in the early financial records as detailed in the 'Book of Reckonings' which covers the period 1500 to 1612. A transcript was compiled in 1963 by the Rev E R Hougham from original manuscripts of the Churchwardens' accounts. These manuscripts are now housed at the Surrey History Centre at Woking but, sadly, are in such a poor state of preservation that inspection is prohibited so we are fortunate to have the Rev Hougham's little gem to fall back on. So how many bells did St James' have when the Book of Reckonings begins in 1500? This is a good time to start as it more or less coincides with the start of the Reformation movement in England.

First, let's consider how many and what sort of bells any parish church would be likely to have in 1500.

Henry VII is on the throne having defeated Richard III at Bosworth Field in the last battle of the Wars of the Roses in 1485 (you know, "A horse, a horse, my kingdom for a horse"). It is said that one Reginald Bray found Richard's crown under a bush and presented it to Henry. The truth of this story may be in some doubt but what is certain is that, as King, Henry granted one of the Shere manors to Reginald, which is still held by the Bray family today.

Try to imagine yourself in the congregation at St James' on a Sunday morning in Henry VII's England in 1500. The first thing to bear in mind is that you are Catholic and St James' is a Catholic church. You really believe in Heaven and Hell and Purgatory. You probably can't read and you have certainly never read the Bible as the only copy in Shere is the one in the church and that is written in Latin. You must rely on the clergy to tell you what the Bible says and to interpret it for you. (It is not until 1536 that Henry VIII decrees that all churches must provide a Bible in English.) The very service is conducted in Latin so, although you learn to appreciate the format, you don't really know what is being said and those at the back probably can't even see the altar.

Shere villagers would be very devout people and it is most important to them that they know at what point in the service they have been represented to their God. This role is fulfilled by sanctus and sacring bells. At the moment of consecration the priest intones "Holy, Holy, Holy," only he is talking in Latin so what he actually says is "Sanctus, Sanctus, Sanctus" and a small sacring bell is rung after each "Sanctus" so it will sound to the congregation as Sanctus...dong, Sanctus...dong, Sanctus...dong.

A sacring bell is a small bell simply rung by hand or, more usually, hung on a rood screen.

The above illustration shows sacring bells being tapped. Note the shape of the bells at this time. Today's bells are more or less harebell shaped – these old bells were rather the shape of a bluebell. Bells hung like this had no clapper and were rung by being tapped with a mallet.

At the same time as the sacring bell was rung, a sanctus bell would be rung. This is a small bell hung in a bell cot on the roof of the church above the chancel, which was used to advise those outside, who are unable to come to the service, that they had been represented to their God.

St James' would, like all other churches at the time, certainly have had a sanctus bell and at least one sacring bell. As well as sanctus and sacring bells a parish church, at this time, could expect to have up to three large bells to be rung, prior to the service, to call the congregation to church.

In 1500 there was a detailed inventory of church assets, so let's see what it tells us. The inventory is recorded in Hougham's transcript of the Book of Reckonings and there is also a partial copy of the original manuscripts done by Philip Palmer in 1913. The inventory is very long and detailed so I have extracted just a few items around the only mention of bells.

Item   a long ladder, vii dussen plates of tree

Item   iiii surpleses, ii Rochette, **iii Sakerying bells**

Item   a lantern, ii small candlestykks for the hye Alter,
v baner poolys, ii supaltares, iiii stavys for the
Crosses, a joined fourme.

A Basin, A long ladder
Seven dozen plates of tree
Four surplices, Two Rochets.
Three sacring bells
Lantern, Two candlesticks for
the High Altar.
Five Banner poles.
Two supaltares for the High
Altar.
Staves for the crosses, joiners
form

Note that Palmer appears to copy exactly from the original, while Hougham lists items in ones and twos without comment on his reasoning. Perhaps Hougham was trying to highlight certain items but I think this masks the situation as it was at the time, so let's follow Palmer. Imagine you are the clerk doing the count. You are walking around the outside of the church and come across a ladder standing against the wall with some roof shingles alongside...so an item. You go into the church and come across a chest or cupboard so you list the contents as an item. Then you come to another cupboard and list these contents as an item; and so on round the church.

Consider first the "ladder and seven dozen plates of tree": in the first place, the ladder will have belonged to the roofer and not to the church; and what a strange logic that you count the shingles waiting to be fitted but do not count the shingles already on the roof.

The next item shows surplices, rochets, and sacring bells in a chest or cupboard, together. This indicates that our sacring bells were simple hand bells and not fixed to a rood screen. How else would they fit into a chest or cupboard?

Whatever differences there may have been between Hougham and Palmer they both agree that St James' had three sacring bells and apparently no other bell of any sort.

As we have seen, the inventory, although detailed, was in fact, not very well done and while St James' might not have had any large bells it would certainly have had a sanctus bell. It seems likely the clerk didn't count anything fixed, or perhaps he had had a long day and was too tired to climb the stairs to the bells!

We have already noted that it is most important that the sanctus bell is rung as the priest intones "Sanctus, Sanctus, Sanctus," and for this reason the ringer of the sanctus bell must have a clear view of the altar.

In many churches the sanctus bell was rung by a clerk pulling a rope from the floor of the church, so there was no problem with seeing the priest. However, if the ringer is hidden in a ringing chamber he would only know when to ring if he had some signal from the priest when the moment arrives, unless he has a spy hole through which he can view the altar.

This brings us to the strange case of the bell ringers' cupboard. This is situated smack in the middle of the east wall of the ringing chamber and is built into the wall itself. I can think of three explanations for such a cupboard:

1. A recess was built into the wall during construction because it was felt that the ringing room, uniquely, required a cupboard.

2. There was no cupboard originally but at some time in the future it was decided the ringing room needed a cupboard and a recess was knocked into the stone wall to accommodate it.

3. A spy hole was designed in the centre of the east wall for the ringer to see the altar. At some time in the future, when it was no longer required, the spy hole was converted into a cupboard.

It doesn't take a Sherlock Holmes to work out which option makes the most sense.

So, in 1500, I believe that St James' had three simple hand bells used as sacring bells and, like all other parish churches, also had a sanctus bell. The sacring bells were rung at exactly the right moment by ringers standing on the floor of the church with a full view of the altar. The sanctus bell was rung by a ringer pulling a rope in the ringing chamber while looking on the altar through a spy hole in the centre of the east wall.

But how many large bells were housed in the bell tower?

Well, in 1552 a further inventory of church property was carried out. This was an official inventory conducted by the church commissioners so we can be fairly sure it was accurate. The very first item in this inventory, as shown in the Book of Reckonings, reads, "In the first place 5 bells, the best by estimation 17 cwt., the next 14 cwt. and so after at that rate." Edward VI was on the throne, having succeeded his father, Henry VIII, in 1547. At this time, the "Protesters", who in the late 15th and early 16th centuries had started by protesting against the sale of indulgencies, began to find more and more to upset them with the Catholic Church, ranging from infant baptism to the very question of the Divinity of Jesus. Edward was a committed 'Protestant' but it was his father, Henry VIII, who had broken with Rome. Henry was not a Protestant, indeed, in 1521 he had written a pamphlet denouncing Lutheranism for which the Pope awarded him the title 'Defender of the Faith'. But Henry desperately wanted a male heir and his queen, Catherine of Aragon, wasn't coming up with the goods. Henry also rather fancied Anne Boleyn so the obvious answer was to divorce Catherine and marry Anne. The Pope wouldn't play ball so Henry declared himself head of the English Church and any clergy who refused to go along were declared guilty of treason. Henry was now in the strange situation where he was executing Protestants for committing heresy at the same time as he was executing Catholics for refusing to accept him as head of the English Church.

If the Book of Reckonings should tell us how many bells were cast between 1500 and 1552 we could calculate how many we had in 1500.

The list opposite shows all items shown in the Rev Hougham's Book of Reckonings between 1500 and 1552 which relate to the bells. I have numbered those that could be a new bell 1 to 5. Looking first at number five in 1547/8, founders were called out but there is no mention of a new bell. Founders would be responsible for bell maintenance and bell frame and wheel maintenance as well as bell casting. There is no mention of making or casting a bell so there seems no reason to believe this was any more than a maintenance call out. Some work was clearly done as 17/- was a substantial sum in 1548.

	1500	Inventory shows Three Sacring Bells
1.	1513	The same delivered to John Eyslett and Rich Mabanke 2/8d to help pay for casting the great bell.

1517   For the bell rope, 11d. For mending the baudrickes, 3d. Paid for a bell rope and line, 1/6d.

2.   1529   Also the wardens have reserved broken silver and the number of 28 pieces with a plate of copper and a crystal stone these made in the year of Our Lord MCCCCCXXIX (1529) according to the aforesaid date.

3.   1529   Delivered to William Risbridger and Robert Smalie, Thomas Hammond and Phillip Francis, wardens for the year, £5.6.8d for making of a bell.

4.   1533   The churchwardens received of Thomas Francis and Robert Parkhurst, roodwardens, of the Church of Shere, four marks of lawful money of England the year 1533, on the 27th of January towards the payment of a new bell.

1536   Whitsun ale made on Whit Sunday, the proceeds 25/2d being mainly devoted to the recasting of one of the bells.

1538   Paid to Master Agate for the mending of bell wheels 4d.

5.   1547/8   Laid out to the messenger to Reading to the bellfounder 2/4d
Laid out in expenses at the time the bellfounder came down 6d.
Paid for mending the fourth clapper 6d.
Paid to the bellfounder by the hands of John Parkhurst 17/-

1552   Official Inventory carried out by Church commissioners:
In the first place 5 bells, the best by estimation 17cwt., the next 4 cwt., and so after at that rate.
1 little sanctus bell.

There can't be much doubt about item 4, in 1533. It talks about four marks towards the payment of a new bell. A mark was worth 13/4d so four marks equates to £2.13.4d (if you don't understand pounds, shillings and pence you will have to take my word for the arithmetic) which, although a substantial sum in medieval England, is not enough to pay for a new bell. However, these church records seem to be recording only the monies that actually went to the church and it is most likely that a local benefactor would have paid the lion's share of the cost. His contribution would probably be paid directly to the founders and therefore need not be recorded. Let's look at items two and three, in 1529, together. Item 2 reports a collection of silver, etc. which Hougham says is for a new bell, while item 3 is quite unequivocal, "£5.6.8d [exactly double the four marks recorded in 1533] for the making of a bell." So is this two bells in 1529? I think not. I believe the collection of silver etc, at item 2, was converted into cash in the sum of £5.6.8d which was then "Delivered to William Risbridger, Robert Smalie, Thomas Hammond and Phillip Francis" who were to be the Churchwardens for the following year. This means that items two and three relate to one bell, probably cast in 1530.

Item 1 talks of casting the great bell. In the 16th Century, the 'great bell' was the normal way of describing the largest bell (now called the tenor). On the face of it, this entry means the 'great' bell was cast in 1513 but there is a problem here. To add a bell to a ring one would normally add one with a higher note than those in situ; the key of the ring is determined by the lowest note (biggest bell), so if one wants to add a larger bell (lower note) one could expect to recast the whole ring. However, if one starts with only two bells I suppose it is possible they are both natural pitch so adding a larger, third bell might be possible. It is a fact that the item in the Book of Reckonings for 1513 clearly states "2/8d for casting the great bell". Maybe, in the 16th Century they talked of making (see item 3) a bell as we would now talk of casting and in 1513 when they spoke of casting they were, in fact, referring to recasting. I could accept that but in 1536 they clearly talk of, "recasting a bell" which indicates they distinguished between casting and recasting. This is a real conundrum but I am advised, by Whitechapel Foundry, that whilst additional bells are usually smaller, so maintaining the keynote, this is a general rule which was frequently broken, so this could be a new bell. I had decided that item 1 did in fact refer to a new bell when the word 'the' was brought to my attention. Would one say, "Casting the bell," if it was a new one? Wouldn't one rather say, "Casting a bell"? I think, probably, one would but this is 'the great bell' and today we talk of the tenor. I simply don't know the answer but I lean towards a new bell. After all, who am I to challenge the accuracy of the churchwarden of 1513? If I am right there were three new bells cast between 1500 and 1552, which by dint of simple arithmetic indicates we had two bells in 1500. So, the best I can say is that it is probable we had two but possible we had three bells in 1500. (See appendix iii.)

There are two other items of interest on the list. You will see that in 1517, 1/6d was paid for something called a "bell rope and line". I have never heard of such a thing and pondered for a long time what it might be. Then I read what Palmer had written. Once again, remember that Palmer is writing an exact copy of the original documents. He lists the same item as a "bell rope and a line". Now this makes a lot more sense. It is not one item but two, purchased from the same supplier, a bell rope and also a line. I think the line may well be a much smaller rope such as would be required for our sanctus bell.

Look now at 1538 when we paid for mending the bell wheels. What a pity it doesn't say how many! In 1538, the wheels would have been half or, possibly, three-quarter wheels. There was no such thing as whole wheel ringing until the 17th century.

The earliest method of ringing large church bells was to hang them from a spindle and then swing the bell against the clapper. More control was achieved, probably towards the end of the 14th century, by fixing the bell to a rimmed quarter wheel. The rope was attached inside the rim, with the spindle acting as a pivot. The rope was pulled, so swinging the bell on to the clapper. The quarter wheel was developed into a half wheel and then a three-quarter wheel. This gave more control but the method of ringing was precisely the same. So our five bells would have been hung on half or three-quarter wheels.

The illustration below shows what a bell on a half wheel would probably have looked like. The bell is hung on a wooden headstock which is attached to a half wheel. The whole would be pivoted on a wooden frame. As you can see, the ringer would pull the rope to swing the half wheel, having the effect of swinging the bell on to the clapper.

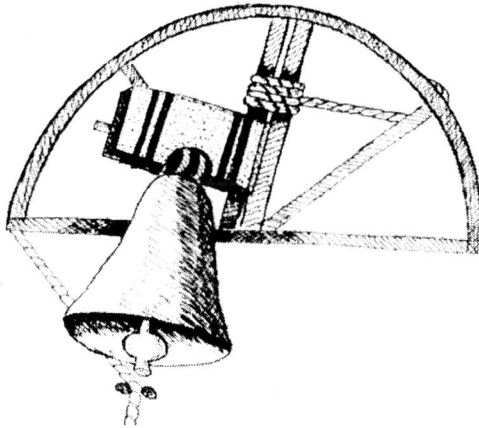

Imagine that you have pulled the rope so the bell is raised to about one o'clock (and eleven o'clock). Ring it much higher and there is a danger of losing control as it swings right over the top. The ringer must first raise the bell to a ringing position. This is a matter of swinging the bell against the clapper and then letting it swing back the other way, under gravity, to strike the clapper again, and continue doing this until the bell is about one o'clock. The ringer has control at the first pull but he must let gravity control the second. Ringing is obviously difficult when you control only every other stroke and even when the bell has been raised to one o'clock, there is no way to stop it.

Henry VIII died in 1547 and his son Edward VI succeeded him at the tender age of nine. The Duke of Somerset was appointed Protector. Edward and Somerset were staunch Protestants and the Reformers, led by Cranmer, began to transform the English Church. In 1549 the 'Act of Uniformity' was passed. Henceforth, the New Book of Common Prayer was to be used. Services were to be conducted in English, superseding Latin. Most congregations could now understand what was being said so there was no need for sacring bells and these and sanctus bells were confiscated by the state.

It must be understood that English was not the language of every Englishman in the mid 16th century. In Cornwall, the majority spoke little English so the argument that Latin was not understood was countered by, "We know as much Latin as English." Consequently, the switch to the use of the English language for church services was not universally accepted. In the north of England and in the West Country particularly, fierce resistance was encountered. This was evidenced by the Western Rebellion of 1549, when Exeter was besieged and the Northern Rebellion of 1569–70. Both were finally put down with many executions.

To a large extent the ease of transition from Catholicism to Protestantism, Latin to English, depended on the personality of the Royal Commissioner appointed for the region. And here it seems the regions most likely to be troublesome had the most belligerent Commissioners assigned to them. These regions would have been the north of England and the West Country. Shere seems to have been fortunate in this respect but it is still rather surprising that we had a sanctus bell in 1552 and I bet it was confiscated pretty quickly.

By 1552 church bell ringing was firmly established in England. Indeed, with thoughts of invasion from the Continent ever present, Bishop Hugh Latimer remarked, "If all the bells in England were rung at one time there would scarcely be a single spot where a bell could not be heard." We are now nearing the end of Edward's short reign. He died in 1553, to be succeeded by Lady Jane Grey who only lasted for nine days before the reign of Bloody Mary was unleashed upon the nation. Mary reigned for five years. She was a devout Catholic and quickly restored Papal supremacy and sanctioned the persecution of Protestants.
For example, she had Hugh Latimer arrested in her first year and burnt at the stake in 1555. On her death in 1558 she was succeeded by Elizabeth I who imposed the Protestant religion by law in 1559.

Eleven years later, in 1570, one Robert Mot established a bell foundry in Whitechapel, London and the Whitechapel Foundry is still in production today. This is the oldest continuous private manufacturing company in the world. Whitechapel cast, among others, the famous Bow bells of St Mary le Bow in Cheapside, the bells of St Clement Danes of "Oranges and Lemons" fame and perhaps the most famous of all, Big Ben. The Whitechapel Foundry contributes to our story but much later.

In 1590, just two short years after the defeat of the Spanish Armada (were Shere bells rung in celebration?), it is recorded, "The parishioners owe to Richard Eldridge the sum of five pounds and for two cwt. of metal." Was this a sixth bell? I think not. Two hundredweights would be nothing like enough metal to cast a bell. The most likely explanation is that Eldridge recast one of the bells. There is always a metal loss on recast so two hundredweights makes some sense in this context.

Local history now falls silent about the bells for 120 years until 1712. I thought I would use this time to explore full circle ringing. How it works and what effect it had.

WHOLE WHEEL OR FULL CIRCLE RINGING

We have seen how control was improved by fixing the bell first to a quarter wheel, then a half wheel and then a three-quarter wheel. It is probable that the five bells at St James' in 1552 were hung on three-quarter wheels. This gave the ringer some control over three-quarters of a turn. Full circle ringing gives control over 360 degrees.

By 1590, it had been obvious for some time that if a bell was fixed to a full wheel then total control could be obtained, except.........well, except that you can't stop the thing. As soon as a means of stopping the bell after turning through 360 degrees was discovered English church bell ringing as we know it today, was born. The answer proved to be very simple.

Look again at the illustration in the introduction and note the stay sticking up on the right hand side of the headstock. Well, the stay together with the slider solved the problem.

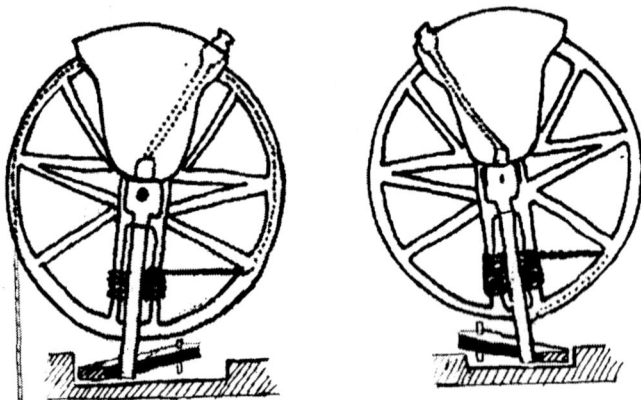

Look at the left hand illustration above. The bell is mouth up with the clapper lying against the back; while at the other end, the stay is resting against a slider. The slider is pivoted at the back and rests in a slider bed which has a stop at each end. The bell is fully supported. Now imagine the bell wheel is pulled anti clockwise. In your mind follow the stay round until it strikes the slider on the other side. The slider, being pivoted at the other end, swings across the slider bed until it reaches the stop. The bell is now fully supported the other way.

I've talked about control but what exactly are we trying to control? Ideally, the gap between each dong should be the same and that is what we are trying to achieve. With half and three-quarter wheels, it was impossible to hold the bell at the top of its swing, gravity would make it fall back whether you liked it or not. So there was no way you could wait for the right moment to pull the rope

With full circle ringing both bell and clapper are stationary each time the ringer pulls the rope. It is significantly easier to control that gap.

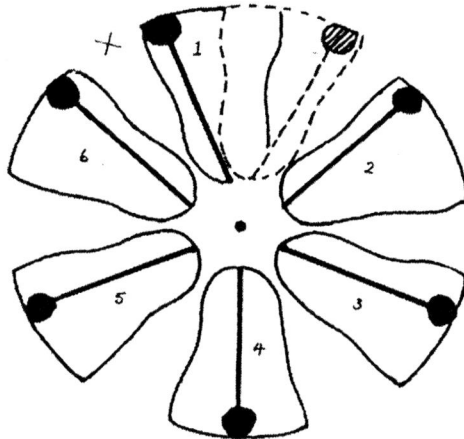

The mechanics of how a bell rings are rather complicated but, put simply, this is what I think happens. We are now going to swing the bell clockwise. Once the bell is pulled off its stop several forces come into play. Two forces affect the bell, namely gravity and the ringer's pull. These same two forces initially affect the clapper to an equal extent. However, the pivot point of the bell is the bearing attached to the bell frame and is fixed and immovable, while the pivot point of the clapper is attached inside the bell and therefore moves with the bell. This extra movement creates an additional force on the clapper which has the effect of making it go faster than the bell. So when the bell starts moving, a race begins. At the outset, the clapper is lying against the back of the bell (1). As the bell rotates, the clapper, moving faster than the bell, gradually leaves the back and catches up with the front (2,3,4,5,6). At about the point marked X, it wins the race....BONG...and then bell and clapper both come to rest in the dotted position. The process is then repeated in the opposite direction. In practice, when the bell is being rung, the ringer checks it just before it reaches the stop and balances the weight of the bell with his, or her, own weight.

THE 17th CENTURY

Throughout the 17th century there is no information about our bells. All we know is that we started the century with five bells and we finished it with five bells. But nationally it was much more exciting.

Guy Fawkes tried blowing up the Houses of Parliament in 1605. He failed and became the first firework night fatality. The 'Mayflower' sailed for America with high hopes and the Pilgrim Fathers in 1620. Oliver Cromwell won the Civil War and executed the King in 1649. The Great Plague, which killed 25% of London's population, was finally stopped by the Great Fire in 1666 but not before the fire had destroyed over 13,000 homes and 87 churches. Samuel Pepys transformed the Navy and wrote a diary.

Did I mention Oliver Cromwell? He decided that no church may have more than two bells capable of being rung. I think it likely he was very conscious of the advantages of their use as a national warning signal but he was a Puritan and Puritans didn't like people having fun. It was obvious that ringers enjoyed ringing but you can't have much fun with two bells. One didn't argue with the New Model Army but no church wanted to destroy perfectly good bells so many resorted to a little subterfuge. The clappers were removed from all but two of the bells. The clappers were then distributed to safe houses within the parish. As St James' finished the century with five bells, Shere must have done something like this but no records were kept so we don't know to which houses or to whom we are indebted.

THE 18th CENTURY

I said earlier that the next mention of the bells is in 1712.

In 1712 Queen Anne is on the throne and it is notable as the year when one Jane Wenham became the last victim to be executed for witchcraft in England.

1712 is important for Shere because it is the year the five bells are recast and, I believe, a sixth added. This information doesn't come from ancient documents, or indeed from any documents at all. The bells themselves tell us. The inscriptions on the bells tell the story. Six of the bells have an inscription indicating they were cast in 1712. Clearly a very major and expensive upgrade took place which was paid for by public subscription. A sixth bell was added thanks to a donation from John Russell whose generosity secures him a place in Shere history by an inscription on the bell. John Russell died the following year and is buried under the nave. The bell he donated would have been, at the time, the smallest, or treble. It is now the third bell as two smaller bells have been added since.

The inscription on the second bell (now the fourth) reads, "R PHELPS FECIT 1712". "T.R; H.M; I.D; I.B; I.B; TB; RIИGERS OF THIS PARISH" (fecit is Latin for 'made'). It is likely that one, at least, of the Bs was a Bignold but I have not discovered who these ringers might be. Maybe this could be an interesting exercise for the future. In this inscription the N of "RINGERS" is in mirror image. No doubt an error by the founder who must inscribe the words on the mould as a mirror image of what appears on the bell. (See appendix ii.)

I believe it is also most likely that it is now that the bells are fitted with whole wheels for full circle ringing. There is no indication when this happened but it seems likely such a major upgrade would be planned at a time of a major refit and this is certainly a major refit. When a bell is added the bell frame itself must be rebuilt so the bells can be arranged in such a way that the various weights complement each other when rung. To neglect this detail could easily result in the bells literally shaking the tower to destruction. If you get a chance to visit the tower when the bells are being rung, take the opportunity to stand against the wall. You will feel the whole tower shaking.

So, I believe that in 1712 the five Shere bells were recast and increased to six in number. A new frame was built to house them and whole wheels fitted. Nowadays, you will often hear just six bells being rung. There are many six bell methods and there are not always eight ringers available competent to ring an eight bell method. On these occasions the six bells that are rung are those recast and rehung in 1712.

An inventory taken in 1714 confirms that, at that time, there are indeed six bells.

John Aubrey, an early historian, wrote in 'The Natural History and Antiquities of the County of Surrey', talking of Shere, "In the tower of this Church is a very fine ring of bells, which the echo of the hills do much ameliorate." The book was published in 1719 by Richard Rawlinson who was a friend of Aubrey. Aubrey had died in 1697 i.e. before the bells were upgraded so, unless Rawlinson added the lines himself, the bells to which Aubrey referred must have been the original five on their half or three-quarter wheels.

There is no further mention of the bells until the next century but it must be said the 18th century was an interesting, if bloody, period. The Duke of Marlborough defeated the French at Blenheim in 1704 and shortly after, in 1715, the Jacobites, assisted by the French, tried unsuccessfully to put the Stuarts back on the throne. They tried again in 1745, culminating in their final defeat at Culloden in 1746. In this battle the English were led by the Duke of Cumberland who was a keen bellringer. The Seven Years' War (we were having trouble with our nearest European neighbour again) ended in 1763 and Canada and India had been added to the Empire. Not a bad result! In 1775 the Americans revolted and finally won their independence in 1783 (aided and abetted by, guess who? Yes, those French again). Six years later came the French Revolution. The revolution didn't make the French any more friendly and by the end of the century we were again having trouble. Now we had Napoleon to contend with but Nelson's victory at the battle of the Nile brought temporary respite.

THE RINGERS

As we have to wait until the 19th century for further information on the bells, I thought we might use this time to look at the early ringers. Frankly, apart from the initials of our six ringers in 1712, the early history of Shere bellringers is nowhere recorded but we do have some idea of the general history of ringers and it seems unlikely the ringers of St James' would have acted very differently from others.

In those early days all ringers would have been men. Quite apart from the fact that women were not expected or encouraged to take up anything so robust, it would have taken strong arms and backs to pull the large bells. There were no such things as ball bearings. So we have a band of men working together in a team doing hard manual work. Hard, thirsty work. Consequently many towers actually had a barrel of beer (not to be confused with small beer which was a low alcohol brew universally drunk in place of water) to keep the ringers going.

A bell in Warwickshire is actually inscribed:

> HARKEN DO YOU HEERE
> OUR CLAPERERS WANT BEERE

Drinking large quantities of beer has an obvious disadvantage for those in the ringing chamber with no easy access to the outside. There are two ways out of the ringing chamber at St James', down the Norman staircase and through the church, or out of the window on to the roof. There can be little doubt that the gutters of St James' often ran with something rather more potent than rain water.

The tradition had grown to ring church bells to celebrate important national and local events and conflict between the clergy and the ringers grew as the clergy tried to control the relevant events and the ringers tried to assert their authority to ring for whatever and whenever they pleased. This conflict grew to real hostility in many parishes. Indeed, to be a ringer in the 18th and early 19th centuries was to be viewed rather worse than we think of lager louts today. An 18th century dictionary defines 'Ringer' as being slang for drunkard. It is difficult to overestimate this hostility. In Mortehoe in Devon, for example, the rector was actually locked out of the tower by the ringers, who changed the lock on the door. There were many instances of clerics refusing a good living on hearing of the reputation of the band of ringers. In theory, the local priest could always assert his obvious authority and if necessary even call the law to his side but in the few instances where the clergy were bold enough to use the law to bring the ringers to heel, they found the congregation took the side of the ringers. The congregation were, after all, the family, friends and workmates of the ringers. This support manifested itself in dwindling congregations with the resulting dramatic drop in the collection.

There are many horror stories of such conflicts but none, I hasten to add, can be found at Shere. It is, of course, not the sort of story the church would happily record for posterity.

We know from churchwardens' accounts that Shere ringers in the late 18th century were, like ringers elsewhere, paid for ringing on special occasions. It is quite clear they didn't have a Trade Union as the rate remained at 5/- for sixty years from 1792 to 1853. Interestingly though, the money wasn't paid directly to the ringers. It was paid to the local publican for beer for them. Beer in the early 19th century cost what? Certainly less than a penny a pint, so 5/- would have bought enough to keep a barrel topped up for a few weeks!

By the end of the 18th century it had become the practice at Shere to ring the bells, apart from service ringing and for weddings and funerals, on three special occasions each year. Namely, the monarch's birthday, coronation day and Guy Fawkes day. On these special occasions the ringers would be reimbursed with 5/- worth of beer. The bells would also be rung for other local and national special occasions which occurred during the year and the ringing band could expect to receive at least £1.5s.0d. worth of beer in any one year.

An answer had to be found to the problems caused by recalcitrant ringers. So it was that in the mid 19th century when Keble's Oxford movement brought a huge development in church refurbishment and maintenance, the means was created to bring the ringers to heel. As maintenance was taking place many churches took the opportunity to remove the floor of the ringing chamber, lengthen the ropes and make the ringers perform from the floor of the church. The ringers were now in full view of the congregation so they had to mind their Ps and Qs. Further, it was no longer possible to slip quietly out of church before the service.

Is this what happened at Shere? Well, there was certainly a period during the 19th century when the bells were rung from the floor of the church, as evidenced by a comment in the Shere Parish Magazine of September 1894 hoping that the ringing chamber will be replaced and stating that the floor had been removed in 1814. Again in 1895 it was reported that "The ringers moved to the floor at the beginning of the century." This is further borne out by the evidence of some receipts of that time which show on 10 May 1799 a charge of £1.6s.0d. for six bell ropes and for a like amount in 1800 and 1802/3. In 1819, however, a set of bell ropes cost £2.14s.0d. Even allowing for inflation this very big increase can only be accounted for by the extra length of the ropes.

We actually have proof that the ringers operated from the floor of the church in the late 19th century, we have a photograph from that time showing the crossing and some of the ropes are clearly visible.

On the left of the above photo you can see three ropes fixed against the wall. You can see the loops where two are tied. On the right, you can just make out another rope. The other two (there were six bells) must be hidden behind the arch.

There is no doubt that some time around 1814 Shere bells were rung from the church floor. This is well before the Oxford movement got going which was some time after 1833, so maybe the Shere clergy were in advance of Oxford. Just maybe, the Shere experiment inspired other churches to follow suit, or perhaps this is all just coincidence. In the absence of further evidence you may make up your own mind. When deliberating you might like to consider that the ringers used to congregate for the Sunday service at the back of the church, in the south west corner, where the bookshelves are now. That area has always been known as sinners' corner.

What is certain is that with the length of the ropes being more than doubled the bells will have been the very devil to handle. The standard of ringing will undoubtedly have fallen significantly. Interestingly, at the end of the 19th century the parish magazine of December 1893 comments that arrangements were made for a Mr W Cumper of Brook to come over to give practical hints to the ringers. It is clear the rector was not happy with the standard of ringing at this time. Standards probably improved when, in June 1894, the Rev C E Matthews joined as a curate. He was a keen ringer and presumably of a high standard as he was elected Secretary of the Winchester Diocesan Guild of Church Bell Ringers in September 1895 (at that time Shere was part of the Winchester Diocese). Matthews actually wrote a hymn to celebrate his good fortune (see appendix iv) Shere ringers must be one of very few bands, possibly unique, to have their own hymn!

Nowadays, the behaviour of the ringers is impeccable but there was a little trouble as close as the 1930s. One Sunday the ringers congregated in their time honoured spot (sinners' corner) and, oh dear, they were caught by the churchwarden, one J E Forrest, playing pontoon. Needless to say, their cards were confiscated.

The present ringers believe strongly that ancient traditions should be upheld which is the only reason why Thursday evening practice sessions always end in a local hostelry.

The present ringers relaxing after a gruelling AGM.

Back row from left: Graham Hughes, Bill Egerton, Jonathan Cross, Eric Thornton, Jane Kumar, John Parker, Anne Patterson, Gabrielle Moss, Mary Kelly. Front row from left: Barbara Norman, Peter Bond, Sally Reay, Virginia Franks.

Not present: Robin Beeson, James Ellenger, John Ellenger, Javed Kumar, Loraine Lawrence.

METHOD RINGING

This seems a good time to have a look at method ringing – which is what we do at St James'.

Because it is necessary to turn the wheel a full circle before it can sound a second time, it is impossible to ring the same note twice in quick succession. For this reason we ring what are called methods rather than tunes. In a method a bell may only be moved one place at a time. Let me explain:

1 2 3 4 **5** 6 7 8   1 2 3 **5** 4 6 7 8   1 2 3 4 6 **5** 7 8

Look at the diagram above and imagine you are ringing the bell number five. If the bells are being rung in the order 1, 2, 3, 4, 5, 6, 7, 8 then the five, which is following the four, may only move to ring over (after) the three or the six; and this rule applies to all the bells all the time. It is not quite so simple as it might seem. It is rare for one bell only to change position. If all bells change one place at the same time, the order would look like this:

2 1 4 3 6 5 8 7

Methods were developed so that bells could be rung in a pattern using this principle. There are literally thousands of methods and at St James' we ring several from time to time, some on six bells and some on all eight. The longest continuous ringing you will have heard is a full peal. This consists of all the possible changes set to the method being rung. A peal of Grandsire Triples, for example, will consist of 5040 changes and take about three hours.

THE 19th CENTURY

Much of the information regarding the 19th century has been covered in the chapter on the ringers. By the end of the 1820s there are problems with the bells, stays and wheels. There are receipts for work done in 1828 for replacement stays and crown staples (the pin holding the bell to the headstock). In 1829 the tenor was causing problems and had become difficult to ring. The wheel was altered (from what to what is unclear) and the bell removed and rehung. There is a bill for "work on various bells February 18, 1829 to October 27, 1830," and during 1831 more work on bell wheels and more crown staples and bolts. The tenor was clearly being a bit of a pig because it was rehung in 1838, as was the third, and there were some repairs to the fifth.

All this work took place after a period of several years when little or no ringing took place. I can find bills for ringers' beer up to 1815 and no further beer until 1818. Remembering that the floor of the ringing chamber was removed in 1814 this may be very significant. 1815 also saw the end of the Napoleonic Wars, which had been fought to keep Napoleonic France at bay. During the twelve years of hostilities the cost of the British Army varied between 60% and 90% of total government income. Much hardship was caused as British commerce was denied access to Continental ports under Napoleon's 'Continental System'. Prices, particularly foodstuffs, rose (inflation is not new) and rose sharply. Jobs were scarce and many people needed financial help to survive. In those days there was no welfare state and the poor were looked after by the parish by the levying of a 'poor rate'. So it may be that there was simply no money available to pay the ringers. We must bear in mind that the records are anything but complete but it seems likely there was a sustained period when the tower was silent. A prolonged period without ringing would cause the bells and their equipment to deteriorate, which may well be why all the work was required. Nevertheless, all work was completed in time to ring for the laying of the first stone of the new school on 24 May 1842, the ringers collecting their 5/- worth of beer.

The records show that by 1818, the ringers' beer, if it had ever been stopped, was restored and I can trace payments until 1852 in which year beer was provided for ringing for Queen Victoria's birthday and coronation day and on 5 November for Guy Fawkes.

There must have been some real problem with the four (now the six) because in 1886 it had to be recast. Gillett & Co. of Croydon, were called in to do the job.

By the end of the century the condition of the bells and bell frame had, once again, deteriorated badly and this made them very difficult to handle. It seems that initially the ringers were blamed for the poor quality of the ringing. As we have seen, Mr Cumper of Brook was called in to train them but, by mid 1894, the poor condition of the bells was recognised and it was decided they should only be rung sparingly.

In 1895, the Whitechapel Bell Foundry (remember them from 1570?) was asked to overhaul the six bells and cast two more. The two new bells are the present treble (one) and the two and were a gift from Miss Georgina Fraser. The previous treble now became the three. In order to add more bells the frame had to be rebuilt and it is likely that parts of the old frame were used. This means that parts of our present frame probably date back to 1712. There was some concern expressed at the time (1895) that the new frame was too flimsy. The main supports are oak beams some 4½ inches x 9 inches and the frame has needed no attention for the last 100 plus years. It was planned that all this work would be completed in time to ring in the New Year but it seems that the ringing chamber floor wasn't actually restored until March 1896.

The first full peal ever rung on Shere bells was in 1896, on the new ring of eight bells, when a peal of Grandsire Triples was rung to celebrate their inauguration.

It is at this time that Ellecombe chimes are fitted. The Rev H T Ellecombe had invented this system in 1860. Essentially, a rope is attached to a hammer which is fixed on the frame below each bell in such a way that when the bell is hanging mouth down and the rope is pulled the hammer strikes the bell. Because the hammer, rather than the bell, is moved it doesn't require a ringer for each bell. In fact, one ringer can ring all eight bells. Because the bell is stationary there is no time delay after it is struck so it can immediately be struck again. This means that it is possible to play simple tunes. If you go into the ringing chamber the Ellecombe ropes can be seen at the far end of the west wall.

With the ringing chamber restored and the ringers no longer performing from the floor of the church now might be a good time to investigate the mystery of the strange grooves on the crossing arch. If you stand immediately below the ringing chamber in the crossing and face west (towards the front door) and look up at the arch above you, you will see several grooves which have obviously been caused by ropes or something similar being rubbed against the stone for a number of years and the story is that these were caused by the bell ropes when the ringers rang from the crossing. If you get the chance to climb right up into the bell loft you will see there is a gap of some two feet between the wall and the bell frame and the ropes are located a further couple of feet away from the wall. Given this gap between the ropes and the wall, it hardly seems possible for even very long ropes to foul the arch. However, it seems that prior to 1895 there was very little gap between the frame and the wall and there is some doubt the bell ropes were arranged in the conventional circle. The Parish Magazine of October 1895, commenting on the work on the bells, states: "The bellropes will fall in a convenient circle and the 8 bells will be so neatly laid in their pits that there will be room to walk all round between the frame and the walls." This would seem to indicate that prior to the re-hanging the bell frame was much closer to the wall than now and the bell ropes were not in a circle. Even if the ropes were not set in the conventional circle, the bells, and presumably the bell ropes, were clearly closer to the wall. Could this and the length of the ropes have caused them to foul the arch?

It occurred to me that when the new frame was built and eight bells set in it, the original rope holes between the bell chamber and the ringing chamber are most unlikely to have been filled in and I could therefore locate the original holes and clear up the matter once and for all. I was able to find one obvious rope hole but no others. The implication is that the original holes now fall beneath the new frame. If this is so, then the ropes would have been at least two feet from the arch. There will certainly be a great deal of flapping about of the ropes when they are 50 or so feet long and normally there will be a guide or guides (a guide is simply a metal spike or screw with a ring at the end) to restrain that swing and such guides would be fitted to the wall. Guides would surely have been fitted but it still leaves an awfully long, unsupported drop.

If the grooves were not made by the bell ropes, the question "What caused them?" needs to be answered. St Andrew's Church at Kinson, Bournemouth is known as the 'smugglers church', so called because in the 19th century smugglers would hide their illicit goods by hauling them up into the ringing chamber. That church has marks very similar to ours, but much deeper, which were caused by the ropes used for hauling. This smuggling can't be blamed on the Kinson ringers because there were none as their bells had been sold in 1797. Smuggling is a most unlikely cause for the Shere grooves so could it have been the bell ropes? I now had another Sherlock Holmes moment and asked myself the question, "What about the grooves that were not made?" We have seen that the ropes were probably much closer to the wall than at present and they were not necessarily laid in a circle, but we know the bells would have been laid such that the movement east to west and north to south is evened out so as not to damage the tower. So, if the bells were close enough to the west wall for the ropes to foul the arch, surely it follows they would be close enough to the east wall for the same problem to occur. Well not necessarily. If the bells near the west wall are swinging east to west and those near the east wall are swinging north to south then no rope would necessarily be close to the east wall. There is a further twist to the story. In 1814 there was, and still is, a clock on the west wall of the bell chamber. This clock needed regular winding and the winding mechanism is on the west wall of the ringing chamber. So if the winding mechanism is on the west wall of the ringing chamber and the floor is removed then a walkway must be left so that the clock can be wound. It seems most likely the walkway would extend right round the tower but as a minimum it would extend from the door at the top of the winding staircase (which is at the west end of the south wall), along the west wall and also along the south wall if access to the bell chamber is to be possible.

The official explanation for removing the floor was that replacement was required and there was no money to pay for it. The cheapest option was simply to remove the floor. The first question that comes to mind is, "How has the floor become so worn as to need replacing?" The ringing chamber is used on two or three occasions each week for a maximum of a couple of hours each time. The floor boards are fixed to rafters just like those in any house. Actually, it is not quite accurate to say the ringing chamber floor boards are fitted to rafters because in the centre of the floor there is a large trap door put there so bells can be lowered if repairs are required.

We have seen that the bell ropes probably did not fall in a circle as they do today, so if we assume they fall in, more or less, two rows of three then it is possible that at least one of the ringers will be standing on the trap door while ringing. The trap door is obviously the weakest part of the floor. So, I don't think the floor was removed at all, the trap door was and this would mean the necessary walkway remained. Now all that is required is to find a way to ensure the bell ropes don't foul the walkway. With the ropes in two rows it is not unreasonable to assume that some at least, will fall in the hole where the trap door was and all that is required is to fix guides to the trap door surround and drop the new, long ropes, through. Let's now make the assumption that the two ropes nearest the west wall actually intruded over the walkway. If a guide is fitted to the outside edge then the ropes will fall at an angle across the walkway. A clear hazard for the poor fellow who has to wind the clock. The answer is obvious. You fix a guide to the wall and drill a hole through the walkway so the ropes drop straight through and fall well away from anyone on the walkway. Such holes must, of necessity, be close to the wall. Close enough for the rope to flap against the arch!

I don't think the grooves can have been caused at any time a ringing chamber was in use, as any hauling would have been through the trap door which is well away from the arches. Our friend Sherlock Holmes remarked that when you have eliminated all other possibilities whatever remains must be the answer – so is it possible that our arches, like our spire frame, are second hand?

Summing up, I do not believe the scoring can have been done at any time we had a ringing room. That only leaves two possibilities: a) between 1814 and 1896 with no ringing chamber floor and the ropes being held close to the wall by guide holes in a walkway, the ropes caused it, or b) the scoring was already present on second hand arches. I would plump for the ropes but they are both good stories.

The 19th century saw Nelson win the battle of Trafalgar (1805), Wellington triumph at Waterloo (1815) and we fought and won the Crimean war (1853–6) with France on our side for once. The Indian Mutiny was put down in 1858. After many failed attempts, Wilberforce, in 1807, finally got a bill for the abolition of the slave trade passed which stopped the trading in slaves and in 1833 slavery was finally abolished throughout the Empire. It is an interesting sign of the times that in 1791 a previous bill for abolition was defeated with much rejoicing. In Bristol there were firework displays and church bells were rung in celebration. The century finished with Britain embroiled in the Boer War. Victoria was on the throne but coming to the end of her long reign. The British Empire was at its peak.

THE 20th CENTURY

Shere bells were rung to celebrate the end of World War I; the parish magazine of August 1919 reports that the bells were rung on 19 July to celebrate the signing of the peace treaty. At the start of World War II, Parliament forbade church bell ringing except to be used as a warning of invasion (Bishop Latimer must have nodded approval from his grave) but in 1942, with the threat of invasion past, Churchill told Field Marshall Alexander that the bells would be rung to celebrate if victory was achieved at El Alamein. The message from Alexander when he reported the 8th army's historic success was "Ring out the bells". Churches throughout Britain rang out the glad tidings and it is recorded that our bells were rung in 1942 to celebrate. They were rung again in 1943 to celebrate total victory in Africa, in 1945, half muffled, for the death of Roosevelt and, of course, for VE and VJ Days.

In 1947 the bells were rehung by Gillett & Johnson of Croydon and were fitted with those new fangled ball bearings which had been developed in the last quarter of the 19th century (their first major use was for the bicycle). In 1975, Whitechapel Foundry was called in for a detailed inspection. They fitted new wheels, new stays and new slider beds and it is at this time that the old elm headstocks are replaced by cast iron. The seven was found to be cracked and was recast. This work took place in 1976.

There was a bit of a fright in 1991 when it was found that the three, four and five were cracked; the three almost from top to bottom. Recasting three bells would have been a very costly business but, fortunately, a company called Soundweld in Cambridge specialise in welding cracked bells. This process is apparently unique in the world but it works and is very cost effective. Consequently it was decided to take this route with the Shere bells. Nowadays the Guildford Diocese has a bell restoration fund to help pay for such repairs and experts to advise, so the ringers decided to remove the faulty bells and take them to Cambridge themselves.

You can imagine this was a major undertaking but today's ringers are made of stern stuff. We first had to remove the bells from their frames and lower them through two trap doors to the floor of the church.

In the picture opposite you see the three, complete with headstock, being lowered into the ringing chamber. It was now we had a rather nasty surprise. The trap from the bell tower to the ringing chamber does not line up with the trap from the ringing chamber to the church. We had over five and a half hundredweights of bell and headstock to move sideways to locate it through the next trap. We were up to the challenge.

Below you see John Parker seated and pushing the bottom of the bell to swing it through the hole. Dick Bird is pushing the top.

It worked, and the bell was lowered to the church floor.

The bell was then loaded into a Land Rover and taken to Cambridge. Then the ringers went through the whole procedure twice more for the two other cracked bells. When the bells had been welded, the ringers collected them from Cambridge, hauled them back up into the tower and refitted them in their frame.

In 1996 we decided to celebrate the centenary of the first peal by copying it. There was one major difference. In 1896 the ringers consisted of one local man plus seven 'experts' brought in. In 1996 the band consisted of seven regular Shere ringers with one outsider. So you see, we have improved!!

Do you believe in fate? The Parish Magazine of April 1896 reports on this first peal that it failed due to conductor error. The conductor is invariably the most experienced and capable ringer so a conductor error is an unlikely way for a peal to fail. Their second attempt succeeded. When we attempted to copy that first peal in 1996, our first attempt also failed due to conductor error. As in 1896 our second attempt succeeded. In 1996 Shere village heard exactly the same sounds as they did a century earlier. That must be living history.

At the end of 1999 the bells were rung to celebrate 2000 years since Christ's birth. It still puzzles me why we should celebrate 2000 years after 1999 years but it was a great party.

The 20th century was marred by two world wars which effectively cost Britain her e——

By the end of the century man had walked on the moon and exploded the hydrogen bomb. Wars continue to be fought all over a world which is in the midst of global warming but, through it all, the bells of Shere ring out their age old greeting.

SOURCES

The Book of Reckonings   - Philip Palmer's copy (1913)
                                    - Rev E R Hougham's interpretation (1963)

      For the early history to 1612.

Discovering Bells and Bellringing – John Camp

      For the cover picture and information on non Shere related history.

History of St James' Church Shere - Compiled by Tim Austin

      For early background information on St James' Church.

If Only They Had Known - Arthur Knapp

      Whence the 'pontoon' story.

In Praise of Bells - John Camp

      Whence the 18th century dictionary definition of "Bellringer" and for most of the
      non Shere related history of bells, bell ringing and bellringers.

Reformation - Diarmaid MacCulloch

      For background information on those troubled times.

Revolt in the West - John Sturt

      For information on the Western Rebellion of 1549.

Shere Museum Archives - Curator, Elizabeth Rich   - Church Records
                                                          - History Society Records
                                                          - Parish Magazines (Historical)
                                                         - W I Scrap Book
                                                          - etc.

      For a wealth of information, particularly 19th and 20th centuries.

Shere Poverty – Ann Noyes

      Whence the information on the poor state of local finances in 1815.

Surrey History Centre, Woking

      For old church records post 1612. In the main, Churchwarden's accounts.

SHERE BELLS

	INSCRIPTION	cwts	qtrs	lbs
Treble	MEARS AND STAINBANK , FOUNDERS LONDON TO THE GLORY OF GOD AND IN MEMORY OF JOHN FRASER OF NETLEY PARK AND HIS WIFE HESTER ANN MAY MOSTYN, OFFERED BY G.A.F. MDCCCXCV ADESTE FIDELES	5	1	2
Two	MEARS AND STAINBANK, WHITECHAPEL FOUNDERS TO THE GLORY OF GOD AND IN MEMORY OF WILLIAM MOSTYN FRASER, ELIZA FRASER, RICHARD AGNEW FRASER, OFFERED BY G.A.F. VENITE ADOREMUS CHRISTUM DOMINUM	5	3	3
Three	RICHARD PHELPS MADE ME 1712 IOHИ RUSSELL BEИEFACTOR	5	1	21
Four	R. PHELPS FECIT 1712 T.R., H.M., I.D., I.B., I.B., T.B. RIИGERS OF THIS PARISH	6	1	19
Five	RICHARD PHELPS MADE ME 1712	7	2	18
Six	GILLETT AND Co, CROYDON CAST 1712, RECAST 1886 R:L ADAMS RECTOR ARTHUR CLAY)) CHURCHWARDENS EDWARD FARHALL) HORA EST, ORA	9	1	10
Seven	RICHARD PHELPS MADE ME 1712 RECAST 1976 WHITECHAPEL	12	3	17
Tenor	MEARS AND STAINBANK WHITECHAPEL FOUNDRY LONDON CAST 1712. RECAST 1895	15	2	8

Swinging North to South:	Treble, 4, 5, Tenor	**Total weight:**	36	1	19
Swinging East to West:	2, 3, 6, 7	**Total weight:**	35	1	23

Bell weights are traditionally given in Imperial measures. If you really must convert them to metric then you need to know that there are 28 lbs in a quarter and 4 quarters in a cwt. 1 lb equals 0.45359237 kilograms. Work it out for yourself.

Appendix ii

1712 Recast

When our five bells were recast in 1712 the original inscriptions, if there were any, were lost. The new inscriptions contained some oddities.

An inscription is pressed into the mould using dies of each letter which must, of necessity, be pressed in reverse (mirror) image of what is to appear on the bell. I think our die-caster may have been dyslexic as every N is in reverse. He managed to get every other letter correct. It wasn't just a straightforward mistake as the anomaly occurs on two bells every time the letter 'N' appears. (See appendix i).

Early scripts had no character 'J' and an 'I' was used instead. It wasn't until 1630 that a 'J' first began to be used for printing in England. It would have taken some years for the 'J' to be universally used and in 1712, our founders, Richard Phelps, had clearly not yet acquired one of those new fangled letters. Thus, the initials of our six ringers are really, TR, HM, JD, JB, JB, TB, and it was John Russell who presented the new bell. Just to be sure, I searched the burial records for fifty years after 1712 and found no one had died with an initial 'I' but there were lots of Johns and James's.

Appendix iii

You will recall that the original trigger for this book was the 1970s handout which stated, categorically, that there were three bells in 1500. The little book "History of St James' Church Shere", edited by Tim Austin, also makes the same assertion.

The book "History of St James' Church" has been reprinted over the years and back in 1949 it was called "The Story of St James' Church." That edition, which, I think, is the first to mention the bells, makes the statement,

> "The Churchwardens' Book [1500–1612] contains many entries relating to the bells, from which it appears that there were three bells in 1500 and two more added by 1529."

Over the years with further reprints, this statement has become a simple

> "There were three bells in 1500."

(Note that the doubt acknowledged by the word 'appears' in 1949 has been dispelled by the current certainty.)

However, the 1949 statement is rather difficult to understand. The author obviously had access to the Churchwardens' Book which formed the basis of Rev Hougham's Book of Reckonings and from that we know there were five bells in the inventory of 1552. It is also a fact that a bell was cast in 1533, four years after 1529, the last noted in the 1949 edition. Taking the facts as stated, three bells in 1500 plus two more by 1529 makes five bells; add the one cast in 1533 and we have six by the time of the inventory in 1552 but that states we have only five! I can only think that the author of the 1949 publication missed the additional bell cast in 1533 and simply deducted the two he had found from the five in the 1533 inventory to arrive at three in 1500. Either that, or he misunderstood what sacring bells are and simply took the three sacring bells as being large church bells and looked for two more to make up the five in 1552. Having found two by 1529, perhaps he simply stopped looking.

It seems likely that further publications simply copied the information in the previous edition and probably the 1970s tower handout copied what the church book asserted.

Rev C E Matthews was appointed curate of St James' Shere in June 1894.

He was appointed Secretary to the Winchester Diocesan Guild of Church Bell Ringers in September 1895 and wrote this hymn, presumably to celebrate. There is no music available but it seems to work to "Oh Happy Band of Pilgrims." I know this hymn was sung at St James' at the beginning of the 20th Century but it has certainly not been sung for the last 25 years.

THE RINGERS' HYMN by Rev C E Matthews

The sacred Bells of England,
How gloriously they ring!
From ancient tower and steeple,
For cottager, for King;
We love to hear their voices
While o'er the fields we roam;
How sweet to think the echo
May reach our Heavenly Home.

Church bells of happy England!
Your songs of olden time
Are chanted down the ages
For Vespers and for Prime!
On merry Christmas morning,
On Holy Easter day
Fulfil your festal calling,
Bid Church folk up and pray.

Church bells of Christian England!
Ring out your message wide,
Whene'er our Lord is blessing
The bridegroom and the bride;
Or when the tenor tolling,
With passing knell we hear,
May one and all remember
A soul to God is near.

Ringers of happy England!
Who peal in earthly fanes
For Christ our Lord and Master
(He all your homage claims),
Complete your sacred office
While pilgrims on this strand,
That ye may swell the praises
In that Eternal Land.

Appendix v

PEALS RUNG AT ST JAMES'

For Winchester Guild 1896–1927

	Date	Method	Time	Comments
1	30/05/1896	Grandsire Triples	3hrs 5m	The 1st peal at Shere
2	20/05/1899	Stedman Triples	2hrs 56m	
3	19/05/1900	Kent Major	3hrs 11m	
4	11/08/1900	Grandsire Triples	3hrs 8m	
5	19/01/1901	Grandsire Triples	3hrs 4m	
6	05/04/1902	Stedman Triples	3hrs 0m	
7	12/09/1903	Grandsire Triples	3hrs 0m	
8	21/10/1903	Grandsire Triples	3hrs 0m	To celebrate anniversary of victory of Trafalgar
9	28/11/1903	Grandsire Triples	2hrs 55m	
10	27/01/1904	Stedman Triples	2hrs 54m	
11	02/07/1904	Double Norwich Major	3hrs 7m	
12	22/02/1905	Grandsire Triples	2hrs 57m	
13	01/07/1905	Double Norwich Major	3hrs 7m	
14	02/09/1905	Grandsire Triples	2hrs 55m	
15	20/05/1907	Superlative Major	3hrs 5m	
16	24/10/1908	Stedman Triples	3hrs 0m	
17	12/11/1909	Grandsire Triples	2hrs 58m	1st by all Shere band for consecration of new part of churchyard and dedication of chancel screen
18	17/03/1923	Kent Major	3hrs 0m	
19	21/06/1924	Plain Bob Major	3hrs 8m	
20	23/10/1926	Grandsire Triples	3hrs 4m	
21	25/06/1927	Grandsire Triples	3hrs 5m	

For Guildford Guild 1928 to date

	Date	Method	Time	Comments
22	12/09/1928	Double Norwich Court Plain Bob Major	3hrs 8m	Silver Wedding of Mr & Mrs Goldsmith
23	09/01/1929	Stedman Triples	3hrs 3m	
24	12/06/1929	Stedman Triples	3hrs 10m	
25	03/01/1931	Grandsire Triples	3hrs 0m	
26	04/05/1940	Kent Treble Bob Major	2hrs 59m	
27	29/09/1945	Grandsire Triples	3hrs 8m	
28	09/04/1949	Grandsire Triples	3hrs 12m	The 1st peal after rehanging
29	08/11/1952	Double Norwich Court Bob Major	3hrs 8m	
30	07/11/1953	Superlative Surprise Major	2hrs 58m	
31	13/09/1969	Plain Bob Major	3hrs 1m	Farewell to David & Margaret James
32	04/03/1978	Grandsire Doubles	2hrs 45m	
33	11/11/1978	Plain Bob Doubles		60th anniversary of Armistice & founding of RAF
34	12/03/1988	Grandsire Triples	3hrs 6m	Surrey Guild Diamond Jubilee
35	04/11/1989	Grandsire Triples	2hrs 59m	80th anniversary of 1st by all Shere band
36	02/03/1991	Plain Bob Doubles	2hrs 42m	Ceasefire in Gulf
37	13/07/1996	Grandsire Triples	2hrs 59m	Centenary of 1st peal
38	24/12/1999	Bristol Surprise Major	3hrs 6m	

INDEX